SELECTED POEMS
STEVIE SMITH

3—

SELECTED POEMS

by Stevie Smith

A NEW DIRECTIONS BOOK

NEW DIRECTIONS BOOKS ARE PUBLISHED FOR JAMES LAUGHLIN
BY NEW DIRECTIONS PUBLISHING CORPORATION,
80 EIGHTH AVENUE, NEW YORK 10011

SIXTH PRINTING

CONTENTS

ACKNOWLEDGEMENTS

We are grateful to Chapman & Hall for permission to include the following poems from their publication *Harold's Leap* by Stevie Smith: The Roman Road; Behind the Knight; Harold's Leap; The Weak Monk; The Ambassador; Le Singe Qui Swing; The After-thought; The Warden; The Death Sentence; Pad, Pad; The Deserter; Thought is Superior; The Orphan Reformed; Cool and Plain; The Wanderer; The River God; My Cats; Oh Stubborn Race of Cadmus' Seed, and Andre Deutsch Ltd. for the following poems from *Not Waving But Drowning* by Stevie Smith: Not Waving But Drowning; The Old Sweet Dove of Wiveton; The Blue from Heaven; 'Come On, Come Back'; Away, Melancholy; In the Park; Fafnir and the Knights; The Airy Christ; The Jungle Husband; I Remember; The Singing Cat; Parents; Songe d'Athalie; The Starling; Childe Rolandine; The Fairy Bell; Why are the Clergy . . .?; The Queen and the Young Princess; Longing for Death because of Feebleness; Loin de l'Etre.

Thoughts about the Person from Porlock

COLERIDGE received the Person from Porlock
And ever after called him a curse,
Then why did he hurry to let him in?
He could have hid in the house.

It was not right of Coleridge in fact it was wrong
(But often we all do wrong)
As the truth is I think he was already stuck
With Kubla Khan.

He was weeping and wailing: I am finished, finished,
I shall never write another word of it,
When along comes the Person from Porlock
And takes the blame for it.

It was not right, it was wrong,
But often we all do wrong.

May we enquire the name of the Person from Porlock?
Why, Porson, didn't you know?
He lived at the bottom of Porlock Hill
So had a long way to go,

He wasn't much in the social sense
Though his grandmother was a Warlock,
One of the Rutlandshire ones I fancy
And nothing to do with Porlock,

And he lived at the bottom of the hill as I said
And had a cat named Flo,
And had a cat named Flo.

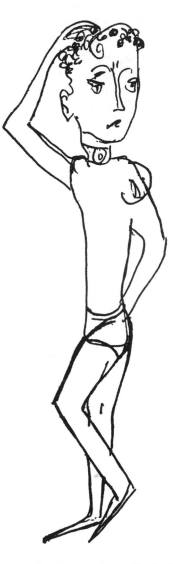

Thoughts about the Person from Porlock (*contd.*)

I long for the Person from Porlock
To bring my thoughts to an end,
I am becoming impatient to see him
I think of him as a friend,

Often I look out of the window
Often I run to the gate
I think, He will come this evening,
I think it is rather late.

I am hungry to be interrupted
For ever and ever amen
O Person from Porlock come quickly
And bring my thoughts to an end.

———————

I felicitate the people who have a Person from Porlock
To break up everything and throw it away
Because then there will be nothing to keep them
And they need not stay.

———————

Why do they grumble so much?
He comes like a benison
They should be glad he has not forgotten them
They might have had to go on.

———————

These thoughts are depressing I know. They are
        depressing,
I wish I was more cheerful, it is more pleasant,
Also it is a duty, we should smile as well as submitting
To the purpose of One Above who is experimenting
With various mixtures of human character which goes
        best,
All is interesting for him it is exciting, but not for us.
There I go again. Smile, smile, and get some work
        to do
Then you will be practically unconscious without
        positively having to go.

Thoughts about the Christian Doctrine
of Eternal Hell

Is it not interesting to see
How the Christians continually
Try to separate themselves in vain
From the doctrine of eternal pain.

They cannot do it,
They are committed to it,
Their Lord said it,
They must believe it.

So the vulnerable body is stretched without pity
On flames for ever.   Is this not pretty?

The religion of Christianity
Is mixed of sweetness and cruelty
Reject this Sweetness, for she wears
A smoky dress out of hell fires.

Who makes a God? Who shows him thus?
It is the Christian religion does,
Oh, oh, have none of it,
Blow it away, have done with it.

This god the Christians show
Out with him, out with him, let him go.

Recognition not Enough

SIN recognised—but that—may keep us humble,
But oh, it keeps us nasty.

Was He Married?

Was he married, did he try
    To support as he grew less fond of them
Wife and family?

No,
He never suffered such a blow.

Did he feel pointless, feeble and distrait,
Unwanted by everyone and in the way?

From his cradle he was purposeful,
His bent strong and his mind full.

Did he love people very much
Yet find them die one day?

He did not love in the human way.

Did he ask how long it would go on,
Wonder if Death could be counted on for an end?

He did not feel like this,
He had a future of bliss.

Did he never feel strong
Pain for being wrong?

He was not wrong, he was right,
He suffered from others', not his own, spite.

But there *is* no suffering like having made a mistake
Because of being of an inferior make.

He was not inferior,
He was superior.

He knew then that power corrupts but some must
    govern?

His thoughts were different.

Did he lack friends?   Worse,
Think it was for his fault, not theirs?

He did not lack friends,
He had disciples he moulded to his ends.

Did he feel over-handicapped sometimes, yet must
    draw even?

How could he feel like this?   He was the King of
    Heaven.

7

. . . find a sudden brightness one day in everything
Because a mood had been conquered, or a sin?

I tell you, he did not sin.

Do only human beings suffer from the irritation
I have mentioned?   learn too that being comical
Does not ameliorate the desperation?

Only human beings feel this,
It is because they are so mixed.

All human beings should have a medal,
A god cannot carry it, he is not able.

A god is Man's doll, you ass,
He makes him up like this on purpose.

He might have made him up worse.

He often has, in the past.

To choose a god of love, as he did and does,
Is a little move then?

Yes, it is.

A larger one will be when men
Love love and hate hate but do not deify them?

It will be a larger one.

Was it not curious?

Was it not curious of Aúgustin
    Saint Aúgustin, Saint Aúgustin,
When he saw the beautiful British children
To say such a curious thing?

He said he must send the gospel, the gospel,
At once to them over the waves
He never said he thought it was wicked
To steal them away for slaves

To steal the children away
To buy and have slavery at all
Oh no, oh no, it was not a thing
That caused him any appal.

Was it not curious of *Gregory*
Rather more than of Aúgustin?
It was not curious so much
As it was wicked of them.

The Frozen Lake

To a mere
   Sir Bedevere
Consigned Excalibur.

White and silent is the snowflake
Falling, falling, and it will make
Soon all flat and like a white lake
In a white and silent state
Beaming flat and vacant.

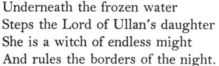

Underneath the frozen water
Steps the Lord of Ullan's daughter
She is a witch of endless might
And rules the borders of the night.

So however white and silent
Seems the lake, it is not vacant
But contains Lord Ullan's daughter
Walking as her Uncle taught her.

Her Uncle is a greater sage
At witchcraft than the lady is
But he has gone, one knows not where
And so his niece only is here.

No, this water is not vacant
But is full of deep intent
Of deep intent and management
Contrived by Ullan's daughter
To what end I know not.

And to my mind the lake is brighter
For the lady's presence; whiter
Though its coat of winter make it
It is for Ullan's daughter's sake it
Beams to me so brightly.

Often as I gaze upon it
Tread upon the ice upon it
I can feel the water shiver
As the lady with a slither
Comes to tap the ice, to tear it,
Yes, I think that I can hear it
Tapped and tickled with her fingers
Where a floe in splinter lingers
Where I cannot come.
But I swear I hear her, seem to
See her face that seems to beam to
Me that hovers half-enchanted
Yes I hover half-enchanted
Wondering if I am wanted
Beckoned by her smile or threatened,
And as always, so today
As I stand and wonder, Ullan's daughter
Goes away.

To a mere
Sir Bedevere
Consigned Excalibur
And who is this who now comes here?
It *is* Sir Bedevere.

This afternoon Sir Bedevere
Found me hesitating by
The icy lake, and he said: Sir,
Where lies the sword Excalibur?

I answered with a lie:
'It must be in some other mere.'
And then I said, 'I truly love her,
Love the Lord of Ullan's daughter
And so I answered with a lie
As I can only think of her.
Oh shall I go beneath the water
Where she walks, or wait for her?
Tell me, Sir Bedevere,
Shall I wait here for her?
He looked at me, but did not say
A word, then he too went away.

And so they go. I am alone,
The white lake beams beneath the moon,
O dear white lake, O dearest love
That will not show yourself above
The bitter ice, but leave me here
To be annoyed by Bedevere,
I come, I come. And then I dived
Into the lake, but through my side
As I went down to seek for her
There passed the sword Excalibur,
In cold and silence seek for her,
The sword sunk in the mere.

And so I died, and the lake-water
That holds the form of Ullan's daughter
With all my blood is dyed,
Is dyed,
With all my love is dyed.

Poor Soul, poor Girl !

(A DEBUTANTE)

I CANNOT imagine anything nicer
Than to be struck by lightning and killed suddenly
    crossing a field
As if somebody cared.
Nobody cares whether I am alive or dead.

From the French

I NDOLENT youth,
 Drawn by everything in turn,
By not being decided enough
I lost my life.

Admire Cranmer!

ADMIRE the old man, admire him, admire him,
   Mocked by the priests of Mary Tudor, given to the
      flames,
Flinching and overcoming the flinching, Cranmer.

Admire the martyrs of Bloody Mary's reign,
In the shocking arithmetic of cruel average, ninety
A year, three-hundred; admire them.

But still I cry: Admire the Archbishop,
The old man, the scholar, admire him.
Not simply, for flinching and overcoming simply,
But for his genius, admire him,
His delicate feelings of genius, admire him,

That wrote the Prayer Book
(Admire him!)
And made the flames burn crueller.   Admire Cranmer!

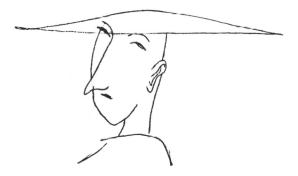

Votaries of Both Sexes Cry First to Venus

Crying for pleasure,
Crying for pain,
Longing to see you
Again and again.

To the tune:
Angels of Jesus,
Angels of light
Singing to welcome
The pilgrims of the night.
(from Hymns A. & M.)

But one stood up and said: I love
The love that comes in the dark fields,
In the late night, in the hot breathless dark night;
In the moony forest, when there is a moon,
In the moony rides of the dark forest.

16

I love this love; it is eerie if there is not
My love in *my* arms then.   It is an excitement
In the arms of a person.   It is exciting then,
It is such an excitement as is on the approach
Of Death; it is *my* love in *my* arms, and then
The trees and the dark trees and the soft grass and the moon
Are not arrogant, as they are if I am alone,
Not a measure, a great measure of indifference, not arrogant
Or in their way exciting either in a way that is too much.

Here this person standing up before Venus wept
And wept, and the tears of this person were warm
And this person then said: There is no love in my arms
No sweet person I love in my arms, and the tears
And the soft strong feelings I parade underneath the trees,
I lay them down; on the soft dark grass I lay down
My strong feelings.   They are for you to eat up, Venus,
But you do not care for them much.   Then they are
For the god who created me.   Let him have them.

Then this person began to laugh and to dance
And Venus was offended; but behind Venus there came
First a little light, then some laughter, then a hand
That took up the great feelings, and then a blessing fell
Like the moon, and there was not any Venus any longer
But the votaries were not abashed, they were blessed

            Crying for pleasure,   (*tune as above*)
            Crying for pain,
            Longing to see you
            Again and again.

Yes this time when they sang their song they were blessed.

Not Waving but Drowning

NOBODY heard him, the dead man,
  But still he lay moaning:
I was much further out than you thought
And not waving but drowning.

Poor chap, he always loved larking
And now he's dead
It must have been too cold for him his heart
      gave way,
They said.

Oh, no no no, it was too cold always
(Still the dead one lay moaning)
I was much too far out all my life
And not waving but drowning.

From the French

"WE shall never be one mummy only
  Beneath the antique deserts and the happy palms."

I Was so Full . . .

I was so full of love and joy
  There was not enough people to love,
So I said: Let there be God,
Then there was God above.

I was so full of anger and hate
To be hated was not enough people,
So I said: Let there be a Devil to hate,
Then down below was the Devil.

These persons have worked very much in my mind
And by being not true, have made me unkind,
So now I say: Away with them, away; we should
Not believe fairy stories if we wish to be good.

Think of them as persons from the fairy wood.

The Old Sweet Dove of Wiveton

'TWAS the voice of the sweet dove
I heard him move
I heard him cry
Love, love.

High in the chestnut tree
Is the nest of the old dove
And there he sits solitary
Crying, Love, love.

The gray of this heavy day
Makes the green of the trees' leaves and the grass
    brighter
And the flowers of the chestnut tree whiter
And whiter the flowers of the high cow-parsley.

So still is the air
So heavy the sky
You can hear the splash
Of the water falling from the green grass
As Red and Honey push by,
The old dogs,
Gone away, gone hunting by the marsh bogs.

Happy the retriever dogs in their pursuit
Happy in bog-mud the busy foot.

Now all is silent, it is silent again
In the sombre day and the beginning soft rain
It is a silence made more actual
By the moan from the high tree that is occasional,

Where in his nest above
Still sits the old dove,
Murmuring solitary
Crying for pain,
Crying most melancholy
Again and again.

From the Italian

(An Old Superstition)

A woolly dog,
A red-haired man,
Better dead
Than to have met 'em.

God Speaks

I MADE Man with too many faults.   Yet I love him.
And if he wishes, I have a home above for him.
I should like him to be happy.   I am genial.
He should not paint me as if I were abominable.
As for instance, that I had a son and gave him for their
    salvation.
This is one of the faults I meant.   It leads to nervous
    prostration.
All the same, there is a difficulty.   I should like him to be
    happy in heaven here,
But he cannot come by wishing.   Only by being already at
    home here.

The Blue from Heaven

(A LEGEND OF KING ARTHUR OF BRITAIN)

K ING ARTHUR rode in another world
And his twelve knights rode behind him
And Guinevere was there
Crying: Arthur, where are you dear?

Why is the King so blue
Why is he this blue colour?
It is because the sun is shining
And he rides under the blue cornflowers.

High wave the cornflowers
That shed the pale blue light
And under the tall cornflowers
Rides King Arthur and his twelve knights.

And Guinevere is there
Crying: Arthur, where are you dear?

First there were twelve knights riding
And then there was only one
And King Arthur said to the one knight,
Be gone.

All I wish for now, said Arthur,
Is the beautiful colour blue
And to ride in the blue sunshine
And Guinevere I do not wish for you.

Oh Lord, said Guinevere
I do not see the colour blue
And I wish to ride where our knights rode,
After you.

Go back, go back, Guinevere,
Go back to the palace, said the King.
So she went back to the palace
And her grief did not seem to her a small thing.

The Queen has returned to the palace
Crying: Arthur, where are you dear?
And everyday she speaks of Arthur's grandeur
To the knights who are there.

That Arthur has fallen from the grandeur
Of his powers all agree
And the falling off of Arthur
Becomes their theme presently.

As if it were only temporarily
And it was not for ever
They speak, but the Queen knows
He will come back never.

Yes, Arthur has passed away
Gladly he has laid down his reigning powers
He has gone to ride in the blue light
Of the peculiar towering cornflowers.

'Come on, Come back'

(*incident in a future war*)

LEFT by the ebbing tide of battle
On the field of Austerlitz
The girl soldier Vaudevue sits
Her fingers tap the ground, she is alone
At midnight in the moonlight she is sitting alone on a
    round flat stone

Graded by the Memel Conference first
Of all humane exterminators
M.L.5.
Has left her just alive
Only her memory is dead for evermore.
She fears and cries, Ah me why am I here?
Sitting alone on a round flat stone on a hummock there.

Rising, staggering, over the ground she goes
Over the seeming miles of rutted meadow
To the margin of a lake
The sand beneath her feet
Is cold and damp and firm to the waves' beat.

Quickly—as a child, an idiot, as one without memory—
She strips her uniform off, strips, stands and plunges
Into the icy waters of the adorable lake.
On the surface of the water lies
A ribbon of white moonlight
The waters on either side of the moony track
Are black as her mind.
Her mind is as secret from her
As the water on which she swims,
As secret as profound as ominous.

Weeping bitterly for her ominous mind, her plight
Up the river of white moonlight she swims
Until a treacherous undercurrent
Seizing her in an icy-amorous embrace
Dives with her, swiftly severing
The waters which close above her head.

An enemy sentinel
Finding the abandoned clothes
Waits for the swimmer's return
('Come on, come back')
Waiting, whiling away the hour
Whittling a shepherd's pipe from the hollow reeds.

In the chill light of dawn
Ring out the pipe's wild notes
'Come on, come back.'

Vaudevue
In the swift and subtle current's close embrace
Sleeps on, stirs not, hears not the familiar tune
Favourite of all the troops of all the armies
Favourite of Vaudevue
For she had sung it too
Marching to Austerlitz,
'Come on, come back.'

Away, Melancholy

Away, melancholy,
Away with it, let it go.

Are not the trees green,
The earth as green?
Does not the wind blow,
Fire leap and the rivers flow?
Away melancholy.

The ant is busy
He carrieth his meat,
All things hurry
To be eaten or eat.
Away, melancholy.

Man, too, hurries,
Eats, couples, buries,
He is an animal also
With a hey ho melancholy,
Away with it, let it go.

Man of all creatures
Is superlative
(Away melancholy)
He of all creatures alone
Raiseth a stone
(Away melancholy)
Into the stone, the god,
Pours what he knows of good
Calling good, God.
Away melancholy, let it go.

Speak not to me of tears,
Tyranny, pox, wars,
Saying, Can God
Stone of man's thought, be good?

Say rather it is enough
That the stuffed
Stone of man's good, growing,
By man's called God.
Away, melancholy, let it go.

Man aspires
To good,
To love
Sighs;

Beaten, corrupted, dying
In his own blood lying
Yet heaves up an eye above
Cries, Love, love.
It is his virtue needs explaining,
Not his failing.

Away, melancholy,
Away with it, let it go.

In the Park

WALKING one day in the park in winter
   I heard two silvered gentlemen talking,
Two old friends, elderly, walking, talking
There by the silver lake mid-pooled black in winter.

'Pray for the Mute who have no word to say,'
Cried the one old gentleman, 'Not because they are dumb,
But they are weak.   And the weak thoughts beating in the
      brain
Generate a sort of heat, yet cannot speak.
Thoughts that are bound without sound
In the tomb of the brain's room, wound.   Pray for the Mute.'

'But' (said his friend), 'see how they swim
Free in the element best loved, so wet; yet breathe
As a visitor to the air come; plunge then, rejoicing more,
Having left it briefly for the visited shore, to come
Home to the wet
Windings that are yet
Best loved though familiar; and oh so right the wet
Stream and the wave; he is their pet.'

Finished, the mild friend
Smiled, put aside his well-tuned hearing instrument
And it seemed
The happiness he spoke of
Irradiated all his members, and his heart
Barked with delight to stress
So much another's happiness.

But which other's?   The sombre first
Speaker reversed
The happy moment; cried again
(Mousing for pain) 'Pray for the Mute' (a tear drops)
'They are like the brute.'

Struck by the shout
That he may not know what it's about
The deaf friend again
Up-ends his hearing instrument to relieve the strain.
What?   Oh shock, ' "Pray for the Mute"?
I thought you said the newt.'

Now which is Christianer pray, of these old friends, the one
     who will say
For pain's sake pray, pray; or the deaf other that rejoices
So much that the cool amphibian
Shall have his happiness, all things rejoicing with him?

But wait: the first speaker now, the old sombre one,
Is penetrated quite by his friend's sun
And, 'Oh blessed you,' he cries, 'to show
So in simplicity what is true.'
All his face is suffused with happy tears and as he weeps he
     sings a happy song,
Happier even than his friend's song was, righting the wrong.
So two, better than one, finally strike truth in this happy song:

'Praise,' cries the weeping softened one, 'Not pray, praise, all
     men,
Praise is the best prayer, the least self's there, that least's
     release.'

Fafnir and the Knights

IN the quiet waters
  Of the forest pool
Fafnir the dragon
His tongue will cool

His tongue will cool
And his muzzle dip
Until the soft waters lave
His muzzle tip

Happy simple creature
In his coat of mail
With a mild bright eye
And a waving tail

Happy the dragon
In the days expended
Before the time had come for dragons
To be hounded

Delivered in their simplicity
To the Knights of the Advancing Band
Who seeing the simple dragon
Must kill him out of hand

The time has not come yet
But must come soon
Meanwhile happy Fafnir
Take thy rest in the afternoon

Take thy rest
Fafnir while thou mayest
In the long grass
Where thou liest

Happy knowing not
In thy simplicity
That the knights have come
To do away with thee.

When thy body shall be torn
And thy lofty spirit
Broken into pieces
For a knight's merit

When thy lifeblood shall be spilt
And thy Being mild
In torment and dismay
To death beguiled

Fafnir, I shall say then,
Thou art better dead
For the knights have burnt thy grass
And thou couldst not have fed.

The Airy Christ

*(After reading **Dr Rieu's** translation of St Mark's Gospel)*

WHO is this that comes in grandeur, coming from the
      blazing East?
This is he we had not thought of, this is he the airy Christ.

Airy, in an airy manner in an airy parkland walking,
Others take him by the hand, lead him, do the talking.

But the Form, the airy One, frowns an airy frown,
What they say he knows must be, but he looks aloofly down,

Looks aloofly at his feet, looks aloofly at his hands,
Knows they must, as prophets say, nailèd be to wooden bands.

As he knows the words he sings, that he sings so happily
Must be changed to working laws, yet sings he ceaselessly.

Those who truly hear the voice, the words, the happy song,
Never shall need working laws to keep from doing wrong.

Deaf men will pretend sometimes they hear the song, the words,
And make excuse to sin extremely; this will be absurd.

Heed it not. Whatever foolish men may do the song is cried
For those who hear, and the sweet singer does not care that he
      was crucified.

For he does not wish that men should love him more than
      anything
Because he died; he only wishes they would hear him sing.

Loin de l'Etre

You don't look at all well, quite loin de l'être in fact,
  Poor pale-face what's the matter, dont they know?
Oh they dont know, but still I dont feel well
Nor ever shall, my name is *Loin de l'Etre*.

They stood on the empty terrace above the precipice
When this conversation took place
Between the affectionate but exasperated friend
And the invalid.   It is not possible to be
Ill and merry, poor *Loin de l'Etre* sighed
And forced a smile, but oh she was so tired.
So tired, called Echo, so tired.

Now pull yourself together, cried the friend,
Together, cried Echo,
I must leave you now for a tick, she said,
Mind you dont get edgy looking at the precipice.
The lovely invalid sighed, Loin de l'être,
And Echo taking the form of a handsome young man
Cried, *Loin de l'Etre* and took her away with him.

The Singing Cat

IT was a little captive cat
  Upon a crowded train
His mistress takes him from his box
  To ease his fretful pain.

She holds him tight upon her knee
  The graceful animal
And all the people look at him
  He is so beautiful.

But oh he pricks and oh he prods
  And turns upon her knee
Then lifteth up his innocent voice
  In plaintive melody.

He lifteth up his innocent voice
  He lifteth up, he singeth
And to each human countenance
  A smile of grace he bringeth.

He lifteth up his innocent paw
  Upon her breast he clingeth
And everybody cries, Behold
  The cat, the cat that singeth.

He lifteth up his innocent voice
  He lifteth up, he singeth
And all the people warm themselves
  In the love his beauty bringeth.

The Jungle Husband

Dearest Evelyn, I often think of you
   Out with the guns in the jungle stew
Yesterday I hittapotamus
I put the measurements down for you but they got lost in
   the fuss
It's not a good thing to drink out here
You know, I've practically given it up dear.
Tomorrow I am going alone a long way
Into the jungle.   It is all grey
But green on top
Only sometimes when a tree has fallen
The sun comes down plop, it is quite appalling.
You never want to go in a jungle pool
In the hot sun, it would be the act of a fool
Because it's always full of anacondas, Evelyn, not looking
   ill-fed
I'll say.   So no more now, from your loving husband,
   Wilfred.

Longing for Death because of Feebleness

Oh would that I were a reliable spirit careering around
Congenially employed and no longer by *feebleness* bound
Oh who would not leave the flesh to become a reliable spirit
Possibly travelling far and acquiring merit.

The Starling

I WILL never leave you darling
To be eaten by the starling
For I love you more than ever
In the wet and stormy weather

Thus to the husband sang the wife
That loved him more than his own life
Oh at these words the husband felt
Each hair rise separate upon his icy pelt.

He let himself down from out his room
He went upon the ancient mountain
And there he quite forgot his gloom
As he trod the torrent's icy fountain.

Cold, cold, icy cold,
Cold, cold, cold I am,
Cold has no place in my wife's warm thought
There she will have me cradled and wraught.
Oh nothing, nothing, nothing I
He cried, that in her thinking does not lie.

Then he doffed his clothes and quickly froze
In the ice of the ancient mountain-side
And there in an icy happy doze
He doth for evermore abide.

Down in the valley waits the wife
That loved him more than his own life
And still she sings, in hope to lure
Him to her side again, Be very sure

I will never leave you darling
To be eaten by the starling
For I love you more than ever
In the wet and stormy weather.

I Remember

IT was my bridal night I remember,
   An old man of seventy-three
I lay with my young bride in my arms,
A girl with t.b.
It was wartime, and overhead
The Germans were making a particularly heavy raid on
      Hampstead.
What rendered the confusion worse, perversely
Our bombers had chosen that moment to set out for Germany.
Harry, do they ever collide?
I do not think it has ever happened,
Oh my bride, my bride.

Songe d'Athalie

(from Racine)

IT was a dream and shouldn't I bother about a dream?
But it goes on you know, tears me rather.
Of course I try to forget it but it will not let me.
Well it was on an extraordinarily dark night at midnight
My mother Queen Jezebel appeared suddenly before me
Looking just as she did the day she died, dressed grandly.
It was her pride you noticed, nothing she had gone through
    touched that
And she still had the look of being most carefully made up
She always made up a lot she didn't want people to know
    how old she was

She spoke: Be warned my daughter, true girl to me, she said,
Do not suppose the cruel God of the Jews has finished with you,
I am come to weep your falling into his hands, my child.
With these appalling words my mother,
This ghost, leant over me stretching out her hands
And I stretched out my hands too to touch her
But what was it, oh this is horrible, what did I touch?
Nothing but the mangled flesh and the breaking bones
Of a body that the dogs tearing quarrelled over.

Why are the Clergy . . . ?

WHY are the clergy of the Church of England
    Always altering the words of the prayers in the Prayer
    Book?
Cranmer's touch was surer than theirs, do they not respect
    him?
For instance last night in church I heard
(I italicise the interpolation)
'The Lord bless you and keep you *and all who are dear unto*
    you'
As the blessing is a congregational blessing and meant to be
This is questionable on theological grounds
But is it not offensive to the ear and also ludicrous?
That 'unto' is a particularly ripe piece of idiocy
Oh how offensive it is. I suppose we shall have next
'Lighten our darkness we beseech thee oh Lord *and the*
    darkness of all who are dear unto us.'
It seems a pity. Does Charity object to the objection?
Then I cry, and not for the first time to that smooth face
Charity, have pity.

The Fairy Bell

A renegade poet, having taken to journalism for more money, is rebuked by his Muse in the form of an old gentleman; he cuts her throat.

A DISMAL bell hung in the belfry
    And clanged a dismal tune
And back and forth the bats did fly
Wherever there was room.

He seemed a melancholy but a reasonable creature,
Yet I could see about his hat as it were this belfry steeple.

The agony through which I go,
He said, is something that you ought to know
And something that you will know too
When I have finished telling you.

He took my hand, I could not choose but stand,
Perhaps for his own sake he should not have done this?
Yet I thought Death was the best prize, if he won this.

Oh, the sad music of the backward and forth
Flying of the bats, pleading for worth,
But in this perhaps again I was wrong—
That there was for him some enjoyment in their song?

It is done now and I cannot trouble to rue it,
I took his gullet in my hand and with my knife cut through it.

But still in my head I sometimes hear the soft tune
Of the belfry bats moaning to find more room
And the ding-dong of that imaginary sound
Is as grateful as a fairy bell tolling by waters drowned.

Childe Rolandine

Dark was the day for Childe Rolandine the artist
When she went to work as a secretary-typist
And as she worked she sang this song
Against oppression and the rule of wrong:

It is the privilege of the rich
To waste the time of the poor
To water with tears in secret
A tree that grows in secret
That bears fruit in secret
That ripened falls to the ground in secret
And manures the parent tree
Oh the wicked tree of hatred and the secret
The sap rising and the tears falling.

Likely also, sang the Childe, my soul will fry in hell
Because of this hatred, while in heaven my employer does well
And why should he not, exacerbating though he be but
        generous
Is it his fault I must work at a work that is tedious?
Oh heaven sweet heaven keep my thoughts in their night den
Do not let them by day be spoken.

But then she sang, Ah why not? tell all, speak, speak,
Silence is vanity, speak for the whole truth's sake.

And rising she took the bugle and put it to her lips, crying:
There is a Spirit feeds on our tears, I give him mine,
Mighty human feelings are his food
Passion and grief and joy his flesh and blood
That he may live and grow fat we daily die
This cropping One is our immortality.

Childe Rolandine bowed her head and in the evening
Drew the picture of the spirit from heaven.

Parents

Parents who barely can afford it
  Should not send their children to public schools ill will
    reward it
That skimping and saving and giving up
That seems so unselfish will buy you a pup
Oh what an ugly biting bow-wow
Well Colonel, how does it go now?
Your son aged twenty-two wears a glittering blazer
His conversation about ponds and ducks, oh happy fool,
Is interrupted to speak of his school
As if at fault he'd allowed
Momentarily that pond to draw him from being proud.
Ah, so hardly won through to it, Colonel,
Is to attach too much importance to it
But he's saved; ponds, duck, fish in dark water
Have a tight hold of him.   It is your daughter
Colonel, who is wholly corrupted.
Women when they are snobbish do not loaf
Look at fish, are not oafish
But are persistently mercenary, cold, scheming and calculating,
This in a young girl is revolting.
Oh beautiful brave mother, the wife of the colonel,
How could you allow your young daughter to become aware
    of the scheming?
If you had not, it might have stayed a mere dreaming
Of palaces and princes, girlish at worst.
Oh to become sensible about social advance at seventeen is
    to be lost.

The Queen and the Young Princess

MOTHER, Mother, let me go
There are so many things I wish to do
My child, the time is not yet ripe
You are not yet ready for life
But what is my life that is to come to be?
Much the same, child, as it has been for me
But Mother you often say you have a headache
Because of the crown you wear for duty's sake
So it is, so it is, a headache I have
And that is what you must grow up to carry to the grave.
But in between Mother do you not enjoy the pleasant weather
And to see the bluebottle and the soft feather?
Ah my child, that joy you speak of must be a pleasure
Of human stature, not the measure
Of animals', who have no glorious duty
To perform, no headache and so cannot see beauty
Up, child, up, embrace the headache and the crown
Marred pleasure's best, shadow makes the sun strong.

Harold's Leap

Harold, are you asleep?
Harold, I remember your leap,
It may have killed you
But it was a brave thing to do.
Two promontories ran high into the sky,
He leapt from one rock to the other
And fell to the sea's smother.
Harold was always afraid to climb high,
But something urged him on,
He felt he should try.
I would not say that he was wrong,
Although he succeeded in doing nothing but die.
Would you?
Ever after that steep
Place was called Harold's Leap.
It was a brave thing to do.

Behind the Knight

BEHIND the Knight sits hooded Care
And as he rides she speaks him fair,
She lays her hand in his sable muff,
Ride he never so fast he'll not cast her off.

My Cats

I LIKE to toss him up and down
A heavy cat weighs half a Crown
With a hey do diddle my cat Brown.

I like to pinch him on the sly
When nobody is passing by
With a hey do diddle my cat Fry.

I like to ruffle up his pride
And watch him skip and turn aside
With a hey do diddle my cat Hyde.

Hey Brown and Fry and Hyde my cats
That sit on tombstones for your mats.

"Oh stubborn race of Cadmus' seed . . ."

IT is the bird of burial
I invoke for my brother's funeral
I throw the dust in Creon's eyes
Not my father is blind but my uncle is
And when they have killed me I will stand in the dark hall
And cry: Orcus, see that my sister does not suffer at all.

The Ambassador

'... known also among the Phoenicians as Casmilus' (Lempriere.)

UNDERNEATH the broad hat is the face of the Ambassador
He rides on a white horse through hell looking two ways.
Doors open before him and shut when he has passed.
He is master of the mysteries and in the market place
He is known.   He stole the trident, the girdle,
The sword, the sceptre and many mechanical instruments.
Thieves honour him.   In the underworld he rides carelessly.
Sometimes he rises into the air and flies silently.

Thought is Superior

THOUGHT is superior to dress and circumstance,
It is thought proud thought that sets the world in a
dance.
And what is the greatest thought since the world begun?
Copernicus's discovery that the earth goes round the sun.

The Deserter

THE world is come upon me, I used to keep it a long way
      off,
But now I have been run over and I am in the hands of the
      hospital staff.
They say as a matter of fact I have not been run over
      it's imagination,
But they all agree I should be kept in bed under observation.
I must say it's very comfortable here, nursie has such nice
      hands,
And every morning the doctor comes and lances my
      tuberculous glands.
He says he does nothing of the sort, but I have my own
      feelings about that,
And what they are if you don't mind I shall continue to
      keep under my hat.
My friend, if you call it a friend, has left me; he says I am
      a deserter to ill health,
And that the things I should think about have made off for
      ever, and so has my wealth.
Portentous ass, what to do about him's no strain
I shall quite simply never speak to the fellow again.

The After-thought

RAPUNZEL Rapunzel let down your hair
It is I your beautiful lover who am here
And when I come up this time I will bring a rope ladder
    with me
And then we can both escape into the dark wood immediately.
This must be one of those things, as Edgar Allan Poe says
    somewhere in a book,
Just because it is perfectly obvious one is certain to overlook.
I wonder sometimes by the way if Poe isn't a bit introspective,
One can stand about getting rather reflective,
But thinking about the way the mind works, you know,
Makes one inactive, one simply doesn't know which way to go;
Like the centipede in the poem who was corrupted by the toad
And ever after never did anything but lie in the middle of the
    road,
Or the old gurus of India I've seen, believe it or not,
Standing seventy-five years on their toes until they dropped.
Or Titurel, for that matter, in his odd doom
Crying: I rejoice because by the mercy of the Saviour I
    continue to live in the tomb.
What's that darling? You can't hear me?
That's odd. I can hear you quite distinctly.

The Warden

(To the tune of: 'They played in the beautiful garden . . .')

THEY played in the beautiful garden
   Those children of high degree,
But she sighed as she swam with the Warden
In the depths of the Zuyder Zee.

Oh why did you take me away
From the children I loved so well?
I had other plans in my heart, dear
For the child of my latest spell.

The Warden has decked her with seaweed,
And shells of an ancient design,
But she sighs as she presses his fingers,
My heart can never be thine.

He sits in the golden chair
With the child he would call his own,
But the beautiful child has expired,
He nurses a sea-green stone.

Le Singe Qui Swing

(to the tune of Green-sleeves)

OUTSIDE the house
    The swinging ape
Swung to and fro,
Swung to and fro,
And when midnight shone so clear
He was still swinging there.

Oh ho the swinging ape,
The happy peaceful animal,
Oh ho the swinging ape,
I love to see him gambol.

The Weak Monk

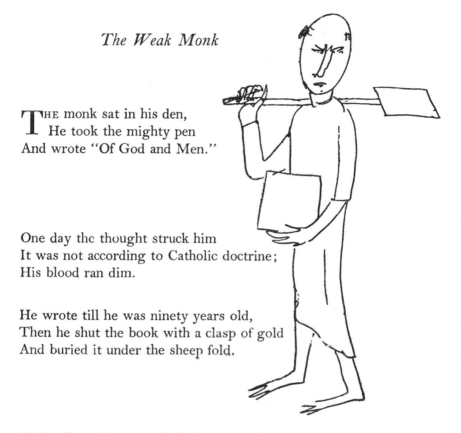

THE monk sat in his den,
  He took the mighty pen
And wrote "Of God and Men."

One day the thought struck him
It was not according to Catholic doctrine;
His blood ran dim.

He wrote till he was ninety years old,
Then he shut the book with a clasp of gold
And buried it under the sheep fold.

He'd enjoyed it so much, he loved to plod,
And he thought he'd a right to expect that God
Would rescue his book alive from the sod.

Of course it rotted in the snow and rain;
No one will ever know now what he wrote of God and men.
For this the monk is to blame.

The Roman Road

A Christian speaks to a Lion in the Arena

OH Lion in a peculiar guise,
Sharp Roman road to Paradise,
Come eat me up, I'll pay thy toll
With all my flesh, and keep my soul.

The Death Sentence

COLD as No Plea,
Yet wild with all negation,
Weeping I come
To my heart's destination,
To my last bed
Between th' unhallowed boards—
The Law allows it
And the Court awards.

Le Majeur Ydow

'EH bien!   Marche!', fit le Majeur Ydow,
'Any more gentlemen like that?   *I'll see them off!*'

But there were no gentlemen really, only the phantoms
He warred with in his perpetual tantrums.

Cool and Plain

Cool and plain
Cool and plain
Was the message of love on the windowpane.
Soft and quiet
Soft and quiet
It vanished away in the fogs of night.

The Conventionalist

Fourteen-year-old, why must you giggle and dote,
Fourteen-year-old, why are you such a goat?
I'm fourteen years old, that is the reason,
I giggle and dote in season.

Pad, Pad

I ALWAYS remember your beautiful flowers
And the beautiful kimono you wore
When you sat on the couch
With that tigerish crouch
And told me you loved me no more.

What I cannot remember is how I felt when you were unkind.
All I know is, if you were unkind now I should not mind.
Ah me, the capacity to feel angry, exaggerated and sad
The years have taken from me.   Softly I go now, pad pad.

The River God

(OF THE RIVER MIMRAM IN HERTFORDSHIRE)

I MAY be smelly and I may be old,
Rough in my pebbles, reedy in my pools,
But where my fish float by I bless their swimming
And I like the people to bathe in me, especially women.
But I can drown the fools
Who bathe too close to the weir, contrary to rules.
And they take a long time drowning
As I throw them up now and then in a spirit of clowning.
Hi yih, yippity-yap, merrily I flow,
O I may be an old foul river but I have plenty of go.
Once there was a lady who was too bold
She bathed in me by the tall black cliff where the water
    runs cold,
So I brought her down here
To be my beautiful dear.
Oh will she stay with me will she stay
This beautiful lady, or will she go away?
She lies in my beautiful deep river bed with many a weed
To hold her, and many a waving reed.
Oh who would guess what a beautiful white face lies there
Waiting for me to smoothe and wash away the fear
She looks at me with.   Hi yih, do not let her
Go.   There is no one on earth who does not forget her
Now.   They say I am a foolish old smelly river
But they do not know of my wide original bed
Where the lady waits, with her golden sleepy head.
If she wishes to go I will not forgive her.

The Wanderer

'TWAS the voice of the Wanderer, I heard her exclaim,
You have weaned me too soon, you must nurse me again,
She taps as she passes at each window pane,
Pray, does she not know that she taps in vain?

Her voice flies away on the midnight wind,
But would she be happier if she were within?
She is happier far where the night winds fall,
And there are no doors and no windows at all.

No man has seen her, this pitiful ghost,
And no woman either, but heard her at most,
Sighing and tapping and sighing again,
You have weaned me too soon, you must nurse me again.

The Orphan Reformed

THE orphan is looking for parents
   She roams the world over
Looking for parents and cover.
She looks at this pair and that
Cries, Father, Mother,
Likes these, does not like those,
Stays for a time; goes,
Crying, Oh hearts of stone.
But really she is better alone.
Orphan, the people who will not be your parents are not evil,
Not the devil.
But still she cries, Father, Mother
Must I be alone for ever?
Yes you must.   Oh wicked orphan, oh rebellion,
Must an orphan not be alone is that your opinion?
At last the orphan is reformed.   Now quite
Alone she goes; now she is right.
Now when she cries, Father, Mother, it is only to please.
Now the people do not mind, now they say she is a mild tease.

O QUEEN of Heaven
  Have pity on me,
My heart is bared
For you to see.

Forgive, forgive
The heart that lies
In anguish bared
Before your eyes.

Mother of God
Behold my heart,
Its sin and stain,
Its bitter smart;

In pity turn
Your pitying gaze
Upon my heart,
And its hopes raze

Quite to the ground,
For there are yet
Some hopes that are
Too highly set.

O lop each hope
And lay it low,
And quench the fire
Of my heart's glow.

For still I hope
He may return,
And while I hope,
Still must I burn

All with desire
That waits on hope
As doth the hangman
On the rope.

Hope and desire,
All unfulfilled,
Have more than rope
And hangman killed.

If I lie down

IF I lie down on my bed I must be here,
But if I lie down in my grave I may be elsewhere.

Girls !

GIRLS! although I am a woman
I always try to appear human

Unlike Miss So-and-So whose greatest pride
Is to remain always in the VI Form and not let down
    the side

Do not sell the pass dear, don't let down the side,
That is what this woman said and a lot of balsy stuff
    beside
(Oh the awful balsy nonsense that this woman cried.)

Girls!   I will let down the side if I get a chance
And I will sell the pass for a couple of pence.

Autumn

HE told his life story to Mrs. Courtly
Who was a widow. 'Let us get married shortly',
He said. 'I am no longer passionate,
But we can have some conversation before it is too late.'

Conviction (1)

CHRIST died for God and me
Upon the crucifixion tree
For God a spoken Word
For me a Sword
For God a hymn of praise
For me eternal days
For God an explanation
For me salvation.

Conviction (2)

I WALKED abroad in Easter Park,
I heard the wild dog's distant bark,
I knew my Lord was risen again,—
Wild dog, wild dog, you bark in vain.

Conviction (3)

THE shadow was so black,
I thought it was a cat,
But once in to it
I knew it
No more black
Than a shadow's back.

Illusion is a freak
Of mind;
The cat's to seek.

The Face

THERE is a face I know too well,
  A face I dread to see,
So vain it is, so eloquent
Of all futility.

It is a human face that hides
A monkey soul within,
That bangs about, that beats a gong,
That makes a horrid din.

Sometimes the monkey soul will sprawl
Athwart the human eyes,
And peering forth, will flesh its pads,
And utter social lies.

So wretched is this face, so vain,
So empty and forlorn,
You well may say that better far
This face had not been born.

Advice to Young Children

'CHILDREN who paddle where the ocean bed shelves
       steeply
Must take great care they do not,
Paddle too deeply.'

Thus spake the awful aging couple
Whose heart the years had turned to rubble.

But the little children, to save any bother,
Let it in at one ear and out at the other.

Edmonton, thy cemetery . . .

EDMONTON, thy cemetery
In which I love to tread
Has roused in me a dreary thought
For all the countless dead,
Ah me, the countless dead.

Yet I believe that one is one
And shall for ever be,
And while I hold to this belief
I walk, oh cemetery,
Thy footpaths happily.

And I believe that two and two
Are but an earthly sum
Whose totalling has no part at all
In heavenly kingdom-come,
I love the dead, I cry, I love
Each happy happy one.

Till Doubt returns with dreary face
And fills my heart with dread
For all the tens and tens and tens
That must make up a hundred,
And I begin to sing with him
As if Belief had never been
Ah me, the countless dead, ah me
The countless countless dead.

The Governess

THE milky love of this bland child
   Her governess has quite beguiled,
And now they spend the hours talking,
Sometimes winding wool and sometimes walking.

Ah, will the Saviour . . . ?

THE cross begot me on the stone,
My heart emits no further moan,
But fortified by funeral thought
Awaits the doom of the distraught.

Ah! will the Saviour never come
To unlock me from the tomb,
To requite the tears that falter
For a birth I could not alter?

The Virtuoso

THE portrait of my mother,
  In plaster lightly scored,
Has always protected me
From anything untoward;
In Manchester or Italy,
Wherever I have toured,
Upon its plinth
It beholds the zenith
Of my success on the pianoforte;
I ask no further reward,
I ask no further reward.

The Heavenly City

I SIGH for the heavenly country,
　Where the heavenly people pass,
And the sea is as quiet as a mirror
Of beautiful beautiful glass.

I walk in the heavenly field,
With lilies and poppies bright,
I am dressed in a heavenly coat
Of polished white.

When I walk in the heavenly parkland
My feet on the pasture are bare,
Tall waves the grass, but no harmful
Creature is there.

At night I fly over the housetops,
And stand on the bright moony beams;
Gold are all heaven's rivers,
And silver her streams.

Love Me !

Love me, Love me, I cried to the rocks and the trees,
And Love me, they cried again, but it was only to tease.
Once I cried Love me to the people, but they fled like a
    dream,
And when I cried Love me to my friend, she began to scream.
Oh why do they leave me, the beautiful people, and only the
    rocks remain,
To cry Love me, as I cry Love me, and Love me again.

On the rock a baked sea-serpent lies,
And his eyelids close tightly over his violent eyes,
And I fear that his eyes will open and confound me with a
    mirthless word,
That the rocks will harp on for ever, and my Love me never
    be heard.

Dirge

From a friend's friend I taste friendship,
  From a friend's friend love,
My spirit in confusion,
Long years I strove,
But now I know that never
Nearer I shall move,
Than a friend's friend to friendship,
To love than a friend's love.

Into the dark night
Resignedly I go,
I am not so afraid of the dark night
As the friends I do not know,
I do not fear the night above
As I fear the friends below.

Study to Deserve Death

STUDY to deserve Death, they only may
Who fought well upon their earthly day,
Who never sheathed their swords or ran away.

See, such a man as this now proudly stands,
Pale in the clasp of Death, and to his hands
Yields up the sword, but keeps the laurel bands

Honour and emulate his warrior soul,
For whom the sonorous death-bells toll;
He after journeying has reached his goal.

Prate not to me of suicide,
Faint heart in battle, not for pride
I say Endure, but that such end denied
Makes welcomer yet the death that's to be died.

Lady 'Rogue' Singleton

COME, wed me, Lady Singleton,
  And we will have a baby soon
And we will live in Edmonton
Where all the friendly people run.

I could never make you happy darling,
Or give you the baby you want,
I would always very much rather, dear,
Live in a tent.

I am not a cold woman, Henry,
But I do not feel for you,
What I feel for the elephants and the miasmas
And the general view.

The Broken Heart

('Oh, Sing to me Gypsy')

HE told me he loved me,
He gave me red roses,
Twelve crimson roses
As red as my blood.

The roses he gave me,
The roses are withered,
Twelve crimson roses
As red as my blood.

The roses are withered,
But here on my breast, far
Redder than they is
The red of my heart's blood.

He told me he loved me,
He gave me red roses,
Twelve crimson roses
As red as my blood.

The Repentance of Lady T

I LOOK in the glass
Whose face do I see?
It is the face
Of Lady T.

I wish to change,
How can that be?
Oh Lamb of God
Change me, change me.

Happiness

HAPPINESS is silent, or speaks equivocally for friends,
Grief is explicit and her song never ends,
Happiness is like England, and will not state a case,
Grief like Guilt rushes in and talks apace.

The Magic Morning

THE boating party
Started at dawn from Clarté.
Lightly lightly they stepped into the green boat
(The Lady Marion has left behind her golden coat).
Marion d'Arcy and Charley Dake
Were the only ones.   He rowed her upon the lake.
He rowed her across the lake until the green shallows
Paled in a waxen lily litter striped with swallows.
And now the morning sun flecks the dark trees
And lightly the mauve sedge moves in a little breeze.

Charley Dake loves the ducal girl
But her eyelids flick flick upon his thoughts' whirl.
Oh my ducal girl, cries Charley in a fit
Of love-spasm.   He is Cupid-hit.
But the Lady Marion smiles and smiles
And so they go again upon the watery miles.

'Oh Charley, Charley, do not go upon the water'
Cries a friendly swan, 'with the Duke's daughter.
You wish to marry er, my boy-carrier? you can not support er
Oh do not go with the Duke's daughter.'

There is an island in the lake, old brick walled,
Where the laurestina climbs and is not spoiled.
What man will spoil the brick walls of their yellow brim?
Such a one as is nervy bold and grim.
(Such a one, says the swan, as has something in store for him.)

Flick flick the eyelids of the lady mark
Where a dark angel floats across her father's park.
All the green grass shivers in a warning,
Flee, Charley, flee the magic morning.

But Charley is folly-blind to the visitation
Of the dark angel of consternation.
Boldly he plucks a golden cup
Throws it in Marion's lap and does not look up.

Ah then the thunder peals and the waters bound
For who took the flower, the angel says, must be drowned.
So up rears the lake water and drags him underneath
Where in suffering he draws his last breath.
'Never more', cries the swan, 'shall Charley be seen,
He is underneath the waters of the mise-en-scène'.
(And 'Charley, Charley, Charley' cry the swan-instructed
    curlews
Ever after as they fly to their nests in the purlieus.)

But the ducal girl comes safe to land and takes her coat,
And goes off in the likeness of a slim stoat.

My Heart was Full

MY heart was full of softening showers,
I used to swing like this for hours,
I did not care for war or death,
I was glad to draw my breath.

Croft

ALOFT,
In the loft,
Sits Croft;
He is soft.

The Pleasures of Friendship

THE pleasures of friendship are exquisite,
   How pleasant to go to a friend on a visit!
I go to my friend, we walk on the grass,
And the hours and minutes like moments pass.

'Après la Politique, la Haine des Bourbons'

COUNT Flanders
Was eaten up with pride;
His dog Sanders
Thought only of his inside.

They were a precious couple,
And let the people feed on straw and rubble.

Bitter was the weather,
Bitter the people,
When they flung Count Flanders
From the church steeple.
Bitter was the weather,
Iron the ground,
When Dog Sanders died of a stomach wound.

Lot's Wife

'In that rich, oil-bearing region, it is probable that Lot's wife was turned into a pillar of asphalt—not salt.' (Sir William Whitebait, Member of the Institute of Mining Engineers.)

I LONG for the desolate valleys,
Where the rivers of asphalt flow,
For here in the streets of the living,
Where my footsteps run to and fro,
Though my smile be never so friendly,
I offend wherever I go.

Yes, here in the land of the living,
Though a marriage be fairly sprung,
And the heart be loving and giving,
In the end it is sure to go wrong.

Then take me to the valley of asphalt,
And turn me to a river of stone,
That no tree may shift to my sighing,
Or breezes convey my moan.

Old Ghosts

'By one half as much power as the Roman Centurion.'
(de Quincey.)

I CAN call up old ghosts, and they will come,
But my art limps,—I cannot send them home.

Satin-Clad

SATIN-CLAD, with many a pearl,
Is this rich and wretched girl.
Does she weep?   Her tears are crystal,
And she counts them as they fall.

Unpopular, lonely and loving

UNPOPULAR, lonely and loving,
  Elinor need not trouble,
For if she were not so loving,
She would not be so miserable.

Hast Du Dich Verirrt?

MY child, my child, watch how he goes,
  The man in Party coloured clothes.

Voices against England in the Night

'ENGLAND, you had better go,
There is nothing else that you ought to do,
You lump of survival value, you are too slow.

'England, you have been here too long,
And the songs you sing are the songs you sung
On a braver day.   Now they are wrong.

'And as you sing the sliver slips from your lips,
And the governing garment sits ridiculously on your hips.
It is a pity that you are still too cunning to make slips.'

Dr. Goebbels, that is the point,
You are a few years too soon with your jaunt,
Time and the moment is not yet England's daunt.

Yes, dreaming Germany, with your Urge and Night,
You must go down before English and American might.
It is well, it is well, cries the peace kite.

Perhaps England our darling will recover her lost thought
We must think sensibly about our victory and not be
        distraught,
Perhaps America will have an idea, and perhaps not.

But they cried: Could not England, once the world's best,
Put off her governing garment and be better dressed
In a shroud, a shroud?   O history turn thy pages fast!

One of Many

You are only one of many
  And of small account if any,
You think about yourself too much.
This touched the child with a quick touch
And worked his mind to such a pitch
He threw his fellows in a ditch.
This little child
That was so mild
Is grown too wild.

Murder in the first degree, cried Old Fury,
Recording the verdict of the jury.

Now they are come to the execution tree.
The gallows stand wide.   Ah me, ah me.

Christ died for sinners, exclaimed the Prison Chaplain
      from his miscellany.
Weeping bitterly the little child cries: I die one of
      many.

'Ceci est digne de gens sans Dieu'
(Allen)

These hands so well articulated
  By brother's life-blood are contaminated
And still he walks, and still the shadows fall,
He clasps them.   There is nothing there at all.

When the Sparrow Flies

WHEN the sparrow flies to the delicate branch
    He seems to be a heavy one alighting there,
It is March, and the fine twigs dance
As the boisterous sparrow plunges masterfully.
Fly again to my heart oh my beloved,
My heart flies too high when you are absent.

Infelice

WALKING swiftly with a dreadful duchess,
   He smiled too briefly, his face was as pale as sand,
He jumped into a taxi when he saw me coming,
Leaving me alone with a private meaning,
He loves me so much, my heart is singing.
Later at the Club when I rang him in the evening
They said: Sir Rat is dining, is dining, is dining,
No Madam, he left no message, ah how his silence speaks,
He loves me too much for words, my heart is singing.
The Pullman seats are here, the tickets for Paris, I am waiting,
Presently the telephone rings, it is his valet speaking,
Sir Rat is called away, to Scotland, his constituents,
(Ah the dreadful duchess, but he loves me best)
Best pleasure to the last, my heart is singing.
One night he came, it was four in the morning,
Walking slowly upstairs, he stands beside my bed,
Dear darling, lie beside me, it is too cold to stand speaking,
He lies down beside me, his face is like the sand,
He is in a sleep of love, my heart is singing.
Sleeping softly softly, in the morning I must wake him,
And waking he murmurs, I only came to sleep.
The words are so sweetly cruel, how deeply he must love me,
I say them to myself aloud, my heart is singing.
Now the sunshine strengthens, it is ten in the morning,
He is so timid in love, he only needs to know,
He is my little child, how can he come if I do not call him?
I will write and tell him everything, I take the pen and write:
I love you so much, my heart is singing.

Brickenden, Hertfordshire

SITTING alone of a summer's evening,
   I thought
Of the tragedy of unwatered country.
O little village of Brickenden,
Where is thy stream,
Translucent drain of thy manorial sward?
Thy sward is green,
Its source of verdancy guessed but unseen.
Where is thy stream?
I have beat every bound of this wild wood.
I have trod down its spiteful and detaining
      undergrowth,
Seeking a broad stream and contented fish,
Seeking but finding not.
Now that the sun
Sou'westering in the sky
Tells me that evening is come,
I rest
Oppressed
By thy wood's profligate viridity,
By thy wood's sap,
Child of a moisture that I cannot tap.

O woods of Brickenden, you have confounded me
By your appearance of humidity.
I see the pashy ground,
And round and round
My tired feet the rushes twine,
And frogs croak and the sweating slime
Is moved by an ambiguous brood
Of low and legless life.

Hadst thou thy stream,
O wood of Brickenden,
This had been
Paradise
But thy sap's virtue comes from dank earth's sweat,
And to be wet
Is not enough, O Wood.
Hadst thou thy stream,
O little village of Brickenden,
Thy stream
Had salined thee
By virtue of destinatory sea,
And thou hadst been
A Paradise.
But lacking stream
Art but a suppuration of earth's humours.
Sitting alone on a summer's evening,
I wept
For the tragedy of unwatered country.
Take thou my tears, O Brickenden,
They are thy rank sweat's sea.

The Failed Spirit

To those who are isolate
War comes, promising respite,
Making what seems to be up to the moment the most
    successful endeavour
Against the fort of the failed spirit that is alone for ever.
Spurious failed spirit, adamantine wasture,
Crop, spirit, crop thy stony pasture!

The Boat

THE boat that took my love away
   He sent again to me
To tell me that he would not sleep
Alone beneath the sea.

The flower and fruit of love are mine
The ant, the fieldmouse and the mole,
But now a tiger prowls without
And claws upon my soul.

Love is not love that wounded bleeds
And bleeding sullies slow.
Come death within my hands and I
Unto my love will go.

Le Désert de l'Amour

I WANT to be your pinkie
I am tender to you
My heart opens like a cactus flower
Do you thinky I will do?

My heart is like a cactus
Not like a cactus flower
And I can kill love
Without entering her bower.

So they both thought.   But he was silent and she said:
I cannot see which way you are pointing, the sky is so dark red,
And when the sandstorm is over I will lie down on my bed.

Mother, among the Dustbins

MOTHER, among the dustbins and the manure
I feel the measure of my humanity, an allure
As of the presence of God.   I am sure

In the dustbins, in the manure, in the cat at play,
Is the presence of God, in a sure way
He moves there.   Mother, what do you say?

I too have felt the presence of God in the broom
I hold, in the cobwebs in the room,
But most of all in the silence of the tomb.

Ah! but that thought that informs the hope of our kind
Is but an empty thing, what lies behind?—
Naught but the vanity of a protesting mind

That would not die.   This is the thought that bounces
Within a conceited head and trounces
Inquiry.   Man is most frivolous when he pronounces.

Well Mother, I shall continue to think as I do,
And I think you would be wise to do so too,
Can you question the folly of man in the creation of God?
        Who are you?

The Deathly Child

THE deathly child is very gay,
   He walks in the sunshine but no shadow falls his way,
He has come to warn us that one must go who would rather
   stay.

Oh deathly child
With a heart of woe
And a smile on your face,
Who is it that must go?

He walks down the avenue, the trees
Have leaves that are silver where they are turned upon the
   breeze.
He is more pale than the silver leaves more pale than these.

He walks delicately,
He has a delicate tread.
Why look, he leaves no mark at all
Where the dust is spread.

Over the café tables the talk is going to and fro,
And the people smile and they frown, but they do not know
That the deathly child walks.   Ah who is it that must go?

The Toll of the Roads

THE angels wept to see poor Tolly dead
He was a harmless simple creature without a thought in
his head.
Oh what is come upon him to make the road his death-bed?

Vater Unser

To the tune of the Londonderry Air

VATER unser,
  Der Du im Himmel wohnst,
Behold thy child,
His prayers and his complaint.
He was conceived
In sin and born to set it on,
This sin is his,
His strength to act upon.
Oh, Father, heed
Thy child, let not the grave
Seal him in sin
Beyond thy power to save.
Strike at his strength,
Leave weakness only for her vaunt,
Vater unser,
Du Der im Himmel wohnst.

The Lads of the Village

THE lads of the village, we read in the lay,
By medalled commanders are muddled away,
And the picture that the poet makes is not very gay.

Poet, let the red blood flow, it makes the pattern better,
And let the tears flow too, and grief stand that is their
begetter,
And let man have his self-forged chain and hug every fetter.

For without the juxtaposition of muddles, medals and clay,
Would the picture be so very much more gay,
Would it not be a frivolous dance upon a summer's day?

Oh sigh no more: Away with the folly of commanders.
That will not take a better song upon the field of Flanders,
Or upon any field of experience where pain makes patterns
the poet slanders.

Nourish Me on an Egg

NOURISH me on an egg, Nanny,
And ply with bottled stout,
And I'll grow to be a man
Before the secret's out.

Nourish me on an egg, Nanny,
With bottled stout to drink,
And I'll grow to be a man
Before you can think.

Nourish me on an egg, Nanny,
Don't wring your hands and weep,
Bring me a glass of stout
And close my eyes in sleep.

I do not Speak

I DO not ask for mercy for understanding for peace
And in these heavy days I do not ask for release
I do not ask that suffering shall cease.

I do not pray to God to let me die
To give an ear attentive to my cry
To pause in his marching and not hurry by.

I do not ask for anything I do not speak
I do not question and I do not seek
I used to in the day when I was weak.

Now I am strong and lapped in sorrow
As in a coat of magic mail and borrow
From Time today and care not for tomorrow.

The Parklands

Through the Parklands, through the Parklands
Of the wild and misty north,
Walked a babe of seven summers
In a maze of infant wrath.

And I wondered and I murmured
And I stayed his restless pace
With a courteous eye I held him
In that unfrequented place.

Questioning I drew him to me
Touched him not but with an eye
Full of awful adult power
Challenged every infant sigh.

'Of what race and of what lineage',
Questioning I held him there,
'Art thou, boy?'   He answered nothing
Only stood in icy stare.

Blue his eyes, his hair a flaxen
White fell gently on the breeze,
White his hair as straw and blue
His eyes as distant summer seas.

Steadfastly I gazed upon him
Gazed upon that infant face
Till the parted lips gave utterance
And he spake in measured pace:

'All abandoned are my father's
Parklands, and my mother's room
Houses but the subtle spider
Busy at her spinning loom.

'Dead my father, dead my mother,
Dead their son, their only child.'
'How is this when thou art living
Foolish boy, in wrath beguiled?'

'Ask me not,' he said, and moving
Passed into the distance dim.
High the sun stood in the heavens,
But no shadow followed him.

The Cousin

STANDING alone on a fence in a spasm,
I behold all life in a microcosm.
Behind me unknown with a beckoning finger
Is the house and well timbered park.   I linger
Uncertain yet whether I should enter, take possession,
    still the nuisance
Of a huge ambition; and below me is the protesting
    face of my cousin.

'I'll have your heart'

I'LL have your heart, if not by gift my knife
Shall carve it out. I'll have your heart, your life.

Flow, Flow, Flow

FLOW, flow, flow,
  Deep river running
To the sea.
Go, go, go,
Let all thy waters go
Over my head,
And when my bones are dead
Long may they lie
Upon the ocean bed,
Thy destiny.

Is it Wise?

Is it wise
To hug misery
To make a song of Melancholy
To weave a garland of sighs
To abandon hope wholly?
No, it is not wise.

Is it wise
To love Mortality
To make a song of Corruptibility
A chain of linked lies
To bind Mutability?
No, it is not wise.

Is it wise
To endure
To call up Old Fury
And Pain for a martyr's dowry
When Death's a prize
Easy to carry?
No, it is not wise.

Upon a Grave

To the tune 'Upon a bank in the greenwood as I lay'

UPON a grave
   In the churchyard as I lay,
An angel out of heaven
Came to me and he did say:
Your child is dead,
He singeth far away,
In Death is sorrow shed,
In Death is sorrow shed.

I raised my head
And mournfully I cried:
My son is dead
I was with him when he died.
He lies alone,
And worms his flesh divide.
In life is sorrow known,
In life is sorrow known.

The Fugitive's Ride

ACROSS the bridge across the dyke
Foresworn by friend and foe alike,
I ride
The field upon the further side
Stretches before me and its wide
Horizon dark against dark sky
Beckons me on.   Dim homesteads lie
To left and right as I ride by.

It is a wet and steamy night,
More steamy night I have not seen
More steamy night there has not been,
I have rode on for many a mile
And now it does not rain
And has not done for quite a while
And all the plain
Lies limpid underneath the stars
That give an eerie light
And make the plain seem to be bright.
With standing water, deep or shallow?
Deep lake, or river?   Corn or fallow?
Lord, Lord, I cannot say
But warily I pick my way
This false starlight is worse than no light
To bewitch
The eyes and hide the gaping ditch.

What owl was that that howls upon
The trees athwart the stream
And have I been this way before
Or do I dream?

He seems to be a mournful one
That hoots to make a coward run
I hate to hear I hate to see
An owl that hoots so dismally
It makes my very blood run cold
No bird should dare to be so bold
I feel as fearful as he should
Who's done a dreadful deed of blood.

(Now hold up horse a moment pray,
Don't sidestep in that foolish way,
If you fall down upon the ground
There is a chance you will be drowned.)

A wetter plain I have not seen
A wetter plain there has not been
I say there has not been
A wetter plain
Since first I came
And may I die
If once again it does not rain.
In early dawn is this dark plain
Made darker still of darkness shorn
More dismaller but still the same
Lit by the ray that heralds day.

On, my poor horse, so lost so wan
That cannot understand
Why we must ride and ride and ride
And never yet come home
On you must go until you drop
For since time won't, I dare not stop.

Private Means is Dead

PRIVATE Means is dead
God rest his soul, officers and fellow-rankers said.

Captive Good, attending Captain Ill
Can tell us quite a lot about the Captain, if he will.

Major Portion
Is a disingenuous person
And as for Major Operation well I guess
We all know what his reputation is.

The crux and Colonel
Of the whole matter
(As you may read in the Journal
If it's not tattered)

Lies in the Generals Collapse, Debility, Panic and Uproar
Who are too old in any case to go to the War.

Bereavement

Maria Holt
Was not the dolt
That people thought her.
Her face was full
Her mind not dull
She was my daughter.
She had so much to do so very much
And used to shuffle round upon a crutch,
The younger children always called her mother,
And so she was to sister and to brother
Poor wretch she's dead and now I am bereft
Of £60 a year to fill the place she left
I never paid a cent before; it is too bad,
It's worse to lose a lass than lose a lad.

Breughel

THE ages blaspheme
The people are weak
As in a dream
They evilly speak.

Their words in a clatter
Of meaningless sound
Without form or matter
Echo around.

The people oh Lord
Are sinful and sad
Prenatally biassed
Grow worser born bad

They sicken oh Lord
They have no strength in them
Oh rouse up my God
And against their will win them.

Must thy lambs to the slaughter
Deliverèd be
With each son and daughter
Irrevocably?

From tower and steeple
Ring out funeral bells
Oh Lord save thy people
They have no help else.

Who Killed Lawless Lean?

THE parrot
Is eating a carrot
In his cage in the garret

Why is the parrot's
Cage in the garret?
He is not a sage
Parrot: his words enrage.

Downstairs
In his bed
Lies the head
Of the family
He is dead.

And the brothers gather
Mutter utter would rather
Forget
The words the parrot
Said.

When high in his cage swinging
From the lofty ceiling
Sat the pet screaming:
'Who killed Lawless Lean?'
It was not at all fitting.

So they put the parrot
In his cage in the garret
And gave him a carrot
To keep him quiet.
He should be glad they did not wring his neck.

Portrait

SHE was not always so unkind I swear
And keep this thought that's all I have of her
Who was upon a time my only thought and care.

Sweet memory, hid from the light of truth
I'll keep thee, for I would not have thy worth
Questioned in Court of Law, nor answer for it on my oath,

But hid in my fond heart I'll carry thee
And to a fair false thought I'll marry thee
And when thy time is done I'll bury thee.

Now Pine-Needles

Now pine-needles
  You lie under the pine-trees
In the darkness of the pine-trees
The sun has not touched you
You are not brown because the sun has touched you
You are brown because you are dead.
The parent tree sighs in the wind
But it does not sigh for sadness
Only because the wind blows
The pine-tree sighs
Only because you are dead
You are brown.
Well, you do not know
That you were so and so
And are now so and so.
So why should I say
You were alive and are now dead
That your parent tree sighs in the wind?
I will sleep on you pine-needles,
Then I shall be
No more than the pine-tree
No more than the pine-tree's needles.

My Muse

My Muse sits forlorn
  She wishes she had not been born
She sits in the cold
No word she says is ever told.

Why does my Muse only speak when she is unhappy?
She does not, I only listen when I am unhappy
When I am happy I live and despise writing
For my Muse this cannot but be dispiriting.